Montessori at Home Guide

101 MONTESSORI-INSPIRED
ACTIVITIES FOR CHILDREN
AGES 2-6

A. M. Sterling

Cover art by: Robert McKinney

Sterling Production
LEXINGTON, KENTUCKY

Sterling Production
www.sterlingproduction.com
ashleyandmitch@sterlingproduction.com

Montessori at Home Guide: 101 Montessori-Inspired Activities for children ages 2-6/ A. M. Sterling —1st ed.
ISBN-13: 978-1537303611
ISBN-10: 1537303619

Contents

This book is dedicated to all the parents who have chosen to honor their children with Montessori learning. The love you have for your child can be shown in no better way than giving them the gift of knowledge.

"Do not tell them how to do it. Show them how to do it and do not say a word. If you tell them, they will watch your lips move. If you show them, they will want to do it themselves."
—DR. MARIA MONTESSORI

Introduction

If you're here looking for Montessori activities for your child, it's very likely that you're already pretty familiar with the Montessori method of education. For that reason, this book does not go into methodology. We would, however, like to offer some basic tips to consider in order to successfully incorporate the activities covered here, into your child's Montessori-inspired learning:

- Remember that children are the great mimickers. For the most part, they learn from what they see adults do. This is why you should demonstrate the activity for them first.
- Breaking the activities down into smaller pieces is a fantastic way to help the child learn. This is especially true if the child is struggling to understand the activity.
- When demonstrating an activity, focus on short, to the point, instructions full of key words. At the age-range, covered in this book, long explanations will do more harm than good.
- Present activities slowly. The child will find a speed, which they are comfortable with, from there.
- Children learn from their mistakes. This is why, in the world of Montessori, we make room for them.

- Present all Montessori activities top to bottom and left to right where it's applicable. This will prepare the child for reading and writing in the future.
- Remember that the child's curiosity is the driving force behind their learning. With this in mind, feel free to deviate from the activities if the child demonstrates curiosity in certain aspects from which they can learn something maybe unintended.
- MAINTAIN A CLUTTER-FREE SPACE. It can't be said enough; clutter in the learning environment equals clutter in the learning.

Many of the activities contained in this book were submitted for inclusion by Montessori bloggers. On their blogs, they give tons of advice on all aspects of Montessori education; more than we could ever fit into this one book. Each activity submitted by one of them will be labeled as such to make it easy to track down the author of your favorites. At the end of this book, we will go further into detail about each Montessori blogger to help you get to know them better. We'd like to encourage you to visit their websites and learn from them, as they are truly valuable resources for your Montessori homeschool.

One other thing of note is that, for each activity in this book, there will soon be released an associated children's story book. Each of the 101 children's story books will be Montessori-inspired and illustrated by the same artist who created the cover art for this book, Robert McKinney. The books will be based on the lives of real children, teaching respect for other cultures. They will contain, not only real life situations that a child can learn from, but the main character in each story will complete an activity from this book to possibly generate interest. We feel that these Montessori-inspired children's story-books will be an excellent complement to the resource we hope this activity book can become for you.

Thank you for your interest in our books and best wishes as you and your child continue down the path of Montessori learning.

Sincerely,
Ashley and Mitch Sterling

Activities

Inspired by
Dr. Maria Montessori

Flower Arrangement

SUBMITTED BY: Diane
www.whenhippostalk.com

SUPPLIES:
- Assortment of flowers
- Vases of different sizes
- Scissors
- Small pitcher
- Funnel (if necessary)
- Sponge
- Paper towel
- Apron
- Basin
- Place mat
- Hand towel
- Doily (optional)

PREPARE:
Select a table to work on and lay out the placemat. Wear an apron.

HOW TO DEMONSTRATE:
Show the child all the materials and lay each one out in a row in the order of use: basin, pitcher, vase, flowers, scissors, paper towel, hand towel, sponge, doily. Add water to the pitcher. Choose a vase and place it in the center of the placemat. Fill the vase with water from

the pitcher. Select a flower. Remove the leaves from the stem and estimate the flower's entire length. Cut the stem so that the flower sits a few inches above the top of the vase. Place the excess stem in the paper towel. Wipe any spills with the sponge. Admire the beautiful new flower arrangement. Take a doily and place it somewhere around the house. Take the vase to where the doily has been set. Repeat until the child is finished with the entire arrangement. Clean up! Fold the paper towel (with the excess stems) and discard. Wipe the scissors in the hand towel. Pour out any excess water from the basin or pitcher. Wipe the basin and funnel with the hand towel. Wipe the placemat with the sponge. Fold the apron and return all the materials to their proper places.

PURPOSE:

Flower arranging allows a child to develop control of movement, logical sequence of action and an eye of aesthetics. It also provides children with opportunities to develop cognitive and fine-motor skills, while developing a sense of independence and confidence in their ability to have a positive impact on their environment.

Magnifying Glass

SUPPLIES:

- Magnifying glass
- Basket
- Collected items to magnify

PREPARE:

The preparation for this activity is actually part of the activity itself: Take the child outside or around the house collecting items to magnify in the basket.

HOW TO DEMONSTRATE ACTIVITY:

Place an item on a well-lit work surface. Hold the magnifying glass a few inches above the item to be looked at. Move the glass and look at item without magnifying. Point out the differences in texture/color/shape, etc. Invite child to do the activity.

PURPOSE:

By exploring the environment then taking a closer look pieces of it, the child's intellectual curiosity is stimulated.

Nuts and Bolts

SUPPLIES:

- Tray
- Two small bowls
- (5) Sets of nuts and bolts that are different sizes (each bolt has only one matching nut that fits)

PREPARE:

Separate the nuts into one bowl and the bolts in another and place the bowls on the tray. Present the activity to the child.

HOW TO DEMONSTRATE:

With the tray on the work surface, lay out the bolts left to right, biggest to smallest. Now, under the bolts, lay out the nuts, left to right, biggest to smallest, matching the proper nut with the proper bolt. Once laid out, begin threading the nuts onto the bolts, left to right. Reset the activity and let the child try.

PURPOSE:

The nuts and bolts activity helps the child with patience. It fine-tunes matching and size identification and practices their precise rotational movements.

Potato Scrubbing

SUBMITTED BY: Anastasia

www.montessorinature.com

SUPPLIES:

- Scrubbing brush
- (2) Bowls
- Dirty potato
- Colander (or strainer)
- Tea towel

PREPARE:

Invite the child to pick necessary tools for potato scrubbing. Fill one bowl with potatoes and another with water, place bowls side by side. Sit the strainer on the side with the towel underneath.

HOW TO DEMONSTRATE:

Demonstrate by picking one potato at a time, moving it above the water and use brush for scrubbing potato. Then place it in a strainer to dry. Invite the child to repeat the process transferring potato from left to right.

PURPOSE:

Direct: scrub dirt off of potatoes for cooking

Indirect: Preparation for writing and reading - repeating left to right pattern of movement, since potato is covered in dirt the child learns that potatoes come from the ground.

Braiding

SUPPLIES:
- A clipboard
- (3+) Different colored strings or yarn
- Tray

PREPARE:
With objects on tray, present to the child.

HOW TO DEMONSTRATE:
Clip the ends of the 3 strings under the clip board. Straighten the strings to be parallel to each other. Perform a simple braid of the strings: Right string over center, left string over the new center string (which started as the right). Repeat. When the child does their braid, you can tie the ends to make a bracelet that the child can wear. Now, let the child try.

PURPOSE:
This is a good dexterity exercise. It teaches braiding and use of logical steps to complete the task.

Baby Doll Washing

SUPPLIES:
- Tray
- A wash cloth
- Child-sized pitcher of water
- Mild baby shampoo
- Dry hand-towel
- Hard plastic baby doll
- Plastic bowl big enough to fit the baby doll in

PREPARE:

Preset the activity with all items on the tray.

HOW TO DEMONSTRATE:

Fill the bowl halfway with water from the pitcher. Put the doll in the bowl to get it wet. Use the baby shampoo and washcloth to wash the baby doll. After washing the doll, place it back in the bowl and pour more water over baby doll to rinse. Use dry hand towel to dry the doll. Reset the activity using fresh water and let child try.

PURPOSE:

The baby doll washing activity helps the child develop their sense of order and cleanliness as well as their pouring skills.

Table Setting

SUPPLIES:
- Tray
- Placemats
- Plates
- Forks
- Spoons
- Knives
- Glasses
- Dining table

PREPARE:
Position all items on the tray for presentation.

HOW TO DEMONSTRATE:
Place the placemats at each position on the table. On each placemat, set a plate in the middle, then a fork to the right side of the plate, a spoon and knife on the left, and a glass to the upper right. Reset all item back to the tray and let the child try.

PURPOSE:
Table setting aids the child in memory development and motor skills.

Preparing Napkins

SUPPLIES:
- Tray
- (10) Napkin rings
- (10) Cloth napkins
- Bowl

PREPARE:
Prepare activity by placing napkins in a stack on the tray, along with the bowl filled with the napkin rings. Present to the child.

HOW TO DEMONSTRATE:
Demonstrate the activity by taking one napkin and rolling it up. Next, place the napkin ring on the rolled napkin. Place the rolled and ringed napkin back on the tray. Prepare all the napkins, rolled and ringed, and stack them neatly on the tray. When finished, reset the activity, separating all the napkins and rings. Let the child try.

PURPOSE:
This activity helps the child develop organizational skills, motor skills, and a sense of order.

Pouring Water

SUBMITTED BY: Diane
www.whenhippostalk.com

SUPPLIES:
- Tray
- (2) Identical glass cups
    - (1) Glass filled half way with water
    - (1) Empty
- Sponge/towel
- Apron

PREPARE:
Prepare for this activity by placing all the items on the tray.

HOW TO DEMONSTRATE:
Show the child how to lift the water glass gently. Then show her also how to angle it over the empty glass. Pour the water out into the empty glass and vice-versa. A sponge or towel can be used to wipe up the spills.

PURPOSE:
This activity involves the use of practical life materials that will develop your child's fine motor skills. Though it is simple, it helps the child's hand-eye coordination, concentration, gracefulness, patience and independence. Repetition is important; encourage her to repeat

the exercise a few times. It will help her master the skills involved and allows her to gain more confidence in herself as well. It will also build the strength and dexterity necessary to hold a pencil appropriately in the future. Don't forget to have her clean up!

Bead Sorting

SUPPLIES:
- Tray
- A medium bowl
- (4) Small bowls
- Beads of 4 different colors

PREPARE:
Prepare the activity by placing all the beads in the medium bowl. Place the medium bowl full of beads and the 4 small bowls on the tray. Present to the child.

HOW TO DEMONSTRATE:
Spread out the 4 small bowls on the table. Pick a bead out of the medium bowl with a pincer grasp and place it in a small bowl. Now pick a different colored bead from the medium bowl and place it in a different small bowl. Do this until every small bowl contains a different colored bead. Continue to pull out beads and sort them by color until the medium bowl is empty and each small bowl contains only beads of one color. Reset the activity by pouring all the beads back into the medium bowl and mixing them up. Now let the child try.

PURPOSE:
Bead sorting aids in the child's development of reasoning skills by way of comparing, sorting, and identification of colors.

Grating Cheese

SUPPLIES:

- Tray
- Cutting board
- Small grater
- Block of cheese (parmesan works good for this)
- Small bowl or sealable container

PREPARE:

Prepare the activity by placing all the objects on the tray. Place the tray on a table that the child can reach.

HOW TO DEMONSTRATE:

Lay the cutting board on the table in front of you. With the cheese block in one hand and the grater in the other, carefully grate the cheese on the cutting board being sure to warn the child to keep their skin away from the grater and to stop when their fingers get too close. Carefully scrape the grated cheese into a pile on the board and put it in the bowl or container. Reset the activity by placing all the objects back on the tray. Let the child try.

PURPOSE:

This activity helps strengthen the hands while developing fine motor skills and understanding object manipulation.

Cleaning Windows

SUPPLIES:
- Small tray
- Nontoxic window cleaner (2 cups water, 2 tablespoons vinegar, 10 drops essential oil)
- Small spray bottle
- Small sponge
- Dry lint-free cloth

PREPARE:

Prepare the activity by filling the spray bottle with cleaner and placing all the items on the tray. Carry the tray to a window or sliding glass door and place on the ground nearby.

HOW TO DEMONSTRATE:

Spray the glass with the nontoxic cleaner. Use the sponge to gently scrub the glass then wipe clean with the cloth. Reset the activity by placing all the items back on the tray and invite the child to try.

PURPOSE:

Cleaning windows helps the child develop motor skills while learning to take care of their environment.

Familiar Faces

SUBMITTED BY: Eloise
www.fridabemighty.com

SUPPLIES:

- Laminated photographs of family members (this can also include family pets) with their names at the bottom of the card such as "dad", "mum", "cat"
- Laminated photograph-only cards
- Laminated name-only cards

PREPARE:

This activity can be presented on a tray, with the cards in three different piles.

HOW TO DEMONSTRATE:

The child should lay out the combination photo and name cards first. Next, they match the photographs to the cards, and then finally match the names. For younger children the name only cards can be left out and the cards can be used as a photo matching exercise. For older children the combination cards can be introduced at the end as a control card, to check they have matched the faces and names correctly.

PURPOSE:

This activity helps early-readers learn name recognition, as well as exposing them to phonetics, and encourages them to read words. The control card ensures that control of error is built into the activity.

Using familiar faces makes this task appealing to even young children.

Rough or Smooth

SUPPLIES:

- Tray
- Piece of coarse sand paper
- Piece of wax paper
- Tape
- Bowl full of rough and smooth objects (jagged and smooth rocks work well for this)

PREPARE:

To prepare, tape the sandpaper down on one side of the tray and the wax paper on the other side, splitting the tray half and half. Set the bowl of rough and smooth objects on top. Present the activity to the child, setting it down on the work surface.

HOW TO DEMONSTRATE:

Feel the coarse sand paper with you finger and say out loud "rough". Next feel the wax paper and say, "smooth". Now pick up an object out of the bowl that is rough. Feel the object with your finger and say "rough" and place it on top of the sandpaper. Next do a smooth object and place it on the wax paper. Continue feeling and sorting until all the objects are sorted. Reset the activity by placing all the objects back in the bowl and let the child try.

PURPOSE:

This activity helps the child develop logically with sorting, using sensorial stimulation.

Nesting Dolls

SUPPLIES:

- Tray
- One set of Nesting dolls

PREPARE:

Present the dolls on the tray.

HOW TO DEMONSTRATE:

Separate the dolls from each other. Line them up on the table, right to left according to size. Open the doll that is next to the smallest, and put the smallest doll inside. Next, open the next larger doll and put the smaller one inside. Continue putting the dolls inside one another slowly, pausing in between each combination to give the child time to process. Once all the dolls are inside the biggest, separate them again and let the child try.

PURPOSE:

This activity helps the child develop a sense of order along with hand-eye coordination.

Changing a Light Bulb

SUPPLIES:
- Tray
- Light bulb
- Small nightlight (one with easy access to the bulb)

PREPARE:
Prepare the activity by placing the light bulb and nightlight on the tray. It may be a good idea to put these items in a bowl to keep the bulb from rolling around. Present to the child.

HOW TO DEMONSTRATE:
Place the activity tray on the work surface. Pick up the small nightlight and carefully unscrew the bulb. Now pick up the new bulb and screw it in carefully. If both bulbs are good there's no need to undo the work you just performed. Just place the items back on the tray and let the child try.

PURPOSE:
This activity aids in developing careful focus and precise rotational movement.

Breakfast is Ready

SUBMITTED BY: Diane
www.whenhippostalk.com

SUPPLIES:

- Cereal scooper
- Cereal container
- Bowl
- Jug (with 1 cup of milk inside)
- Spoon

PREPARE:

Prepare for this activity simply by having all items at the ready.

HOW TO DEMONSTRATE:

Place the milk jug on the table. Show the child the location of the cereal container. Have her carry it to the table. Retrieve a bowl and place it on the table. Show the child how to open the lid of the container. Show her how to take the scooper and dig into the cereal. Place the cereal into the bowl and have the child repeat scooping a few more times until the bowl is filled. Close the cereal container and return it to the shelf. Have her take the jug and slowly pour the milk into the bowl. Get a spoon from the drawer and enjoy. (Note: It's very important that you - as the adult - demonstrate each of these steps before allowing the child to perform them. This practice sets clear goals and expectations. Repeat often if necessary - they will get it.)

PURPOSE:

This task may seem really simple for an adult, but for a child, this is a remarkable achievement. He is learning how to follow directions, control his movements, care for his needs and the needs of others and perform this task with grace. He learns to be patient, careful and gentle while exercising both gross and fine motor skills.

Opening Locks

SUPPLIES:

- Tray
- (4) Padlocks in various sizes labeled 1,2,3, and 4, locked together in a daisy chain
- Keys (not labeled)
- Small basket

PREPARE:

Place all items on tray and present to the child.

HOW TO DEMONSTRATE:

Lay the daisy chained locks on the table. Pick up a key and try to open the first lock labeled '1'. If it doesn't work, try another until you find the correct key and unlock the lock. Once unlocked, lay it to the side with the correct key. Now find the correct key to open lock number 2 and set it aside. Do this in order, 1,2,3, and 4, until all the locks are unlocked with their correct keys. Reset the activity by locking all the locks back together and jumbling the keys. Let the child try.

PURPOSE:

The opening locks activity develops the child's motor skills, familiarizes them with locks and keys, and helps them understand numerical order.

Moving Rice

SUPPLIES:
- Tray
- (2) Small bowls
- (20) Grains of rice
- Tweezers

PREPARE:

Place the 2 small bowls on the tray, 1 containing the rice and 1 empty, along with the tweezers. Present to child.

HOW TO DEMONSTRATE:

Set tray on work surface. User tweezers to move each grain of rice to the previously empty bowl until all the rice has been moved. Now let the child try.

PURPOSE:

This activity helps develop the child's patience with practicing the manipulation of small objects, and tunes their fine motor skills.

Stringing Beads

SUPPLIES:

- Tray
- Shoe lace
- Clothes pin
- Wooden beads in a bowl or pouch

PREPARE:

Place all items on tray and present to child.

HOW TO DEMONSTRATE:

Pick up the shoelace and the cloths pin. Open the pin and allow it to close on one end of the lace. String all of the beads onto the lace, one by one, until the lace is full. Now carefully hold both ends of the lace and adjust the cloths pin so that it now holds both ends together. Now it is a necklace that can be worn safely without the worry of it getting caught on anything. Reset the activity and let the child try.

PURPOSE:

Stringing beads aids in the development of fine motor skills as well as logical thought related to order of operations.

Matching Mittens

SUPPLIES:

- (5) Pairs of mittens
- Small basket

PREPARE:

Place all mittens at random in small basket.

HOW TO DEMONSTRATE:

Bring basket full of mittens to the work area. Take out one of each mitten and lay it on work surface, left to right. Take out the other five mittens, one by one, and lay each mitten on top of its matching one. Fold the mittens appropriately and place in basket. Reset the activity and let the child try.

PURPOSE:

This activity helps the child develop their sense of order and matching skills while teaching care of their environment.

Candleholder Flags

SUBMITTED BY: Mars

www.montessorionmars.com

SUPPLIES:

- Tray
- Multi-candle holder
- Flags (1 per hole in holder)

PREPARE:

Prepare by placing all items on tray.

HOW TO DEMONSTRATE:

Place tray on work surface. Remove a flag and insert it into the candleholder so that it is standing straight up. Do this with the rest of the flags one by one until they are all standing up in the candleholder. Reset the activity and let the child try.

PURPOSE:

This simple activity helps young children develop motor skills and builds confidence.

Inflating a Balloon

SUPPLIES:

- Tray
- Hand-pump
- (2) Small balloons
- Safety glasses

PREPARE:

Present the activity with the hand-pump, safety glasses, and balloons on the tray.

HOW TO DEMONSTRATE:

Place activity on work surface. Put your safety glasses on to protect your eyes in case of over-inflation. Pick up the pump and a balloon and place the mouth of the balloon over the air nozzle of the pump. Hold the mouth firmly on the nozzle with one hand and pump with the other, inflating the balloon. Once the balloon is pumped up reasonably, pinch the mouth of the balloon and remove from the nozzle. Lay down the pump, hold out the balloon, and release it so that the balloon goes flying through the air. Now let the child try.

PURPOSE:

This activity, while for the upper age range of children, is scientific in nature as well as a strength exercise for the hands and arms.

Matching Jar Lids

SUPPLIES:
- Tray
- (4) Jars of different sizes with lids

PREPARE:
Prepare the activity by placing all items on the tray with jar lids off the jars and set to one side, jars on the other. Present to the child.

HOW TO DEMONSTRATE:
Bring the tray activity to the work area. Set out the jars in a line left to right. Now pick up a lid and try it on each jar unit it fits and screw in on. Continue until each jar has a lid. Reset the activity and let the child try.

PURPOSE:
Matching jar lids helps the child develop a sense of order and matching with size differentiation. Also, this activity works on the child's rotational movement skills.

Banana Slicing

SUBMITTED BY: Diane
www.whenhippostalk.com

SUPPLIES:
- Placemat
- Sponge
- Serving Bowl
- Banana
- Cutting board
- Knife
- Fork
- Apron

PREPARE:
Put the placemat at the center of the table. Wear an apron.

HOW TO DEMONSTRATE:
Lay out the materials and introduce each one to the child: cutting board, banana, knife, fork, bowl, sponge. Place the cutting board on the center of the placemat. Show the child how to peel the banana; have her continue until the entire banana is peeled. Place the banana at the center of the cutting board. Pick up the knife by pinching the handle near the teeth of the knife with your right thumb and index finger. Wrap your middle, ring and pinky fingers around the handle — demonstrate for the child first then allow the child to try inde-

pendently. Position your index finger so it rests on the top part of the knife. Hold the banana with your left hand and place your fingers adjacent to the location of the cut. Insert the blade of the knife into the banana and cut in a sawing motion. Continue to cut in this manner until the entire banana has been sliced. Use a fork to place the bananas into the bowl. Serve and enjoy. Clean up! Place the knife, cutting board, fork and bowl in the sink. Wet the sponge and wipe the placemat.

PURPOSE:

This exercise encourages control of movement, a logical sequence of action and a care for the self and others. It equips your child to make herself a snack and serve others. As he gains more confidence in his knife skills, he will be able to prepare other fruits and vegetables such as apples, carrots and cucumbers.

Sorting Silverware

SUPPLIES:

- Tray
- (4) Regular spoons
- (4) Regular forks
- (4) Regular butter knives
- Utensil caddy or drawer insert
- Small bucket

PREPARE:

Place forks, knives, and spoons in bucket randomly. Place bucket and utensil caddy on tray. Preset to the child.

HOW TO DEMONSTRATE:

Bring the tray activity to work area. Begin by pulling one item (maybe a fork) from the bucket and place it in the proper spot in the caddy. Next, pull a different item from the bucket and place it into its proper caddy location. Do this, one at a time, until all utensils are in their proper locations in the caddy. Now reset the activity and let the child try.

PURPOSE:

This activity helps the child learn to recognize similar objects and care of their environment.

Pencil Sharpening

SUPPLIES:
- Small tray
- Small plastic bowl
- Small plastic hand pencil sharpener
- Unsharpened pencils

PREPARE:
Place all the items on the tray and present to the child.

HOW TO DEMONSTRATE:
Carry the tray to mat or table. Pick up a pencil that needs sharpening with non-dominant hand. Hold pencil sharpener in dominate hand over small plastic bowl. Demonstrate twisting motion to sharpen pencil, allowing shavings to drop in bowl. Invite child to try.

PURPOSE:
Pencil sharpening helps teach the child a life-skill, and develops fine motor skills.

Color Patterns using Legos

SUBMITTED BY: Christine

www.ultimatemontessoriparentsguide.com

SUPPLIES:

- Tray
- Small basket or bowl
- Empty egg carton
- (12) Different colored Lego blocks
- Piece of paper
- Crayons or colored pencils
- Tape
- Scissors

PREPARE:

Pick out 12 Lego blocks of different colors and put them in the basket or bowl. Using the scissors cut the piece of paper into a rectangle that will just fit into the lid of the egg carton. On the piece of paper, use the crayons or colored pencils to draw squares that represents blocks in one of the egg locations, coloring them to match the color of blocks you have picked out. This is your Lego map and when you are finished, you will have drawn 12 Lego squares on the map for the 12 egg positions. Tape the map on the inner-top of the egg carton with your block drawings facing out. Place your basket or bowl of Legos and the modified egg carton on the tray.

HOW TO DEMONSTRATE:

Take the tray to the work surface. Open the egg carton. Pick up a Lego and place in in one of the egg indentions in accordance with the positioning of the Lego drawing in the top of the carton. Make sure to match the correctly colored Lego with the correct color of the Lego on the Lego map for that position. Do this until all the egg indentions are filled with Legos. Now reset the activity and let the child try.

PURPOSE:

This color-matching activity uses the child's logic to match the Lego to its correct position. It is an introduction to using a map.

Washing Apples

SUPPLIES:

- Small plastic bucket
- Small pitcher of water
- Washcloth
- (2) Dry towels
- A few apples

PREPARE:

Present all the items on a work surface that is water resistant.

HOW TO DEMONSTRATE:

Spread out one dry towel on the table. With the small pitcher, pour some water in the bucket. Dunk the apple in the water to get it wet. Dunk the washcloth to get it wet as well, then use it to scrub all the surfaces of an apple. Dunk the apple one more time then wipe it dry with one dry towel and set it down on the one that is spread out on the table. Now let the child try the rest of the apples.

PURPOSE:

This activity helps the child learn to care for the environment and the importance of cleanliness; especially of our food.

Walking a Line with a Bell

SUBMITTED BY: Marnie
www.carrotsareorange.com *Carrots are Orange*

SUPPLIES:
- Small basket
- Masking or duct tape to create the "line"
- Bell with string attached

PREPARE:
Create a line on the floor approximately the width of a child's shoe with the masking or duct tape.

HOW TO DEMONSTRATE:
Practice walking the line once without anything in your hands and no shoes. Next take the bell out of the basket and hold in one hand. While balancing the bell out to your side, walk the line. Invite the child to take off their shoes and try it.

PURPOSE:
This activity helps the child learn concentration, balance, calmness and grace. It also aids with the child's gross motor skills.

Planting a Seed

SUPPLIES:

- Tray
- Pack of favorite plant seeds
- (2) Small pots containing soil
- Small watering can full of water
- Paper towel for clean up

PREPARE:

Place all items on the tray.

HOW TO DEMONSTRATE:

Place the tray on the work surface. Using your finger, poke a small hole in the soil. Carefully place 2-3 seeds inside the hole and cover up with soil. Wipe your finger with the paper towel and water the soil just until it is moist. Now let the child try with the other pot. Set both pots on a window ledge, water more when dry, and watch you plants grow!

PURPOSE:

Besides teaching care with fragile things and improving fine-motor skills, this scientific activity helps to familiarize your child with plants and their life-cycles.

Scooping Eggs

SUPPLIES:

- Tray
- Small scoop or spoon
- Two small bowls
- (4) Hard-boiled eggs

PREPARE:

Prepare this activity by placing the eggs in one bowl. Put the bowl with eggs, the empty bowl, and the small scoop on the tray.

HOW TO DEMONSTRATE:

Place activity on the work surface. Use the scoop to scoop up one egg at a time from one bowl and place in the other gently without dropping or cracking.

PURPOSE:

This activity helps the child learn to control of a wobbly object using scoop or spoon as well as working on their fine motor skills.

Object Matching

SUBMITTED BY: Marnie
www.carrotsareorange.com *Carrots are Orange*

SUPPLIES:

- Basket containing multiple pairs of matching objects (Sarari Toobs are perfect as well as household items or pretend fruits and vegetables)
- Large mat

PREPARE:

Prepare the basket of matching objects. Invite the child to do the work. Point out that a large mat is needed. Take objects to rug.

HOW TO DEMONSTRATE:

Take out objects one at a time, naming as you go along. Place in horizontal line. Have the child repeat the names of the objects. Use the 3 period lesson. Remove the second set of objects. Child names each object. Teacher scans objects to find the match. Place under corresponding object. Continue with child. If a child doesn't remember the name of an object, review again. Place objects back in basket and place on shelf.

PURPOSE:

This activity helps improve the child's vocabulary, object discrimination, and memory skills.

Bobbing for Cherries

SUPPLIES:
- Large bowl filled ¾ with water
- A few cherries
- Towel
- Tongs

HOW TO DEMONSTRATE:
Place large bowl of water on a water resistant table. Pour in the cherries. Spread the towel out on the table next to the bowl. Using the tongs, pick the cherries out of the bowl, one by one, setting each cherry on the towel, until they are all out. Reset the activity by placing all the cherries back in the water. Invite the child to try.

PURPOSE:
Bobbing for cherries helps the child to develop concentration and fine motor skills.

Excavation

SUPPLIES:

- Flour
- Paper shreds
- Large flower pot
- Old tooth brushes
- Hand shovels
- Plastic animals
- Rocks
- Bucket
- Water

PREPARE:

Prepare the activity by mixing equal parts of flour and water in the bucket. Make sure your mixture is enough to fill the flower pot at least half way. Next, mix together the paper shreds and the flour/water mixture. Now put some of your shred/flour/water mixture in the bottom of the flowerpot. Grab a plastic animal or two and put them on top. Cover with another layer of mixture, then another animal plus a rock or two. Continue layering until the pot is full and all the objects are buried. Set the activity out in the warm weather to dry for a couple of days.

HOW TO DEMONSTRATE:

Using the hand shovels, carefully dig at the material until you find the first buried item. Us the old toothbrushes to brush off extra debris from the item. Now let your child at it with all the tools to dig and explore.

PURPOSE:

This scientific exploration activity helps to develop patience and fine motor skills. It plays on many children's natural tendency to dig and investigate.

Sink or Float

SUPPLIES:
- Tray
- Small bowl of water
- Basket full of a few common items such as: small pine-cones, sponges, feathers, buttons, rocks, cherries, etc.
- Piece of paper with two categories written on each half, 'sink' on one half and 'float' written on the other (laminating the paper is a big help).

PREPARE:

Present with all items on the tray. Set tray down on water resistant work surface.

HOW TO DEMONSTRATE ACTIVITY:

Pick items out of the basket and place them into small bowl of water one at a time. Watch to see if item sinks or floats. Lay item on 'sink' or 'float' side of paper. Invite child to try activity.

PURPOSE:

The sink or float helps the child learn scientific concepts about the behavior of water and how it interacts with objects.

Using Screwdrivers

SUPPLIES:
- Tray
- (2) Small basket
- Variety of Screws
- Screwdrivers matching the screw heads
- (4) Pieces of cardboard cut into medium sized squares

PREPARE:

Place all screws in on basket and the screwdrivers in another. Place the baskets on the tray along with the cardboard pieces and present to the child.

HOW TO DEMONSTRATE ACTIVITY:

Stack the pieces of cardboard on top of each other neatly. Take a screw and find the proper screwdriver. Hold the screw in place, with the pointed end on top of the stack of cardboard. Take the screwdriver with your dominant hand, place the end on the screw head, and twist the screw down into the cardboard pieces until it is all the way in. Do this until all the screws are in the cardboard. Hold up the stack to demonstrate that the pieces of cardboard are now held together as one. Reset the activity and let the child try.

PURPOSE:

Helps the child learn the life-skill of using screwdrivers while using matching, fine-tuning motor skills and logical thinking.

Emptying the Dishwasher

SUBMITTED BY: Diane
www.whenhippostalk.com

SUPPLIES:

- Dishwasher
- Dishes (clean)
- Cups
- Drawer or low shelves

PREPARE:

Show your child the dishwater. Teach her how to open it and pull out the dish rack. Open the drawer where the respective dishes and cups should be stored.

HOW TO DEMONSTRATE:

Have your child take the dish (using two hands of course) and carry it over to its respective drawer. Repeat until all the dishes and cups are removed from the dishwasher. Believe it or not, your child will be able to clear out the entire dishwasher regularly. Have faith and keep your expectations high and your child will meet or even exceed them.

PURPOSE:

This task fosters a child's interest in helping others and being part of a community. It teaches her a sense of responsibility, grace and control of movement. This also builds confidence and independence.

Folding Washcloths

SUPPLIES:
- Basket
- (10) Square washcloths

PREPARE:

Present the activity with all the washcloths in the basket.

HOW TO DEMONSTRATE ACTIVITY:

Set the basket down at the work area and pull out one cloth. Fold the cloth in half, lining up the edges. Now fold it in half again, once again lining up the edges. Place folded cloth to the side and fold the next one. Place it on top of the previously folded cloth to form a neat stack. Continue for a stack of 5, and then start a new stack. When you are finished with all the cloths you should have 2 neat stacks of washcloths piled 5 high. Reset the activity by messing up all your washcloths and putting them back in the basket. Now let the child try.

PURPOSE:

In this activity, the child learns a life skill while developing concentration and patience. It also teaches care and upkeep of the surroundings as well as a sense of community.

Pizza-cutter

SUPPLIES:

- Tray
- (4) Soft flour or corn tortillas
- Pizza-cutter
- Food coloring marker
- Cutting board
- Small plastic ruler

PREPARE:

On one tortilla, using the food-coloring marker and ruler, draw a line that goes directly down the middle, edge to edge. On one side of the line, draw a number '1' and on the other draw the number '2'. On the next tortilla draw two lines, forming a plus sign in the middle, dividing the tortilla into four equal pieces. Now, on each piece draw a '1', then a '2', then '3', then '4'. On the next tortilla draw four lines, dividing the tortilla into eight equal pieces and number them '1'-'8'. Do this on one more tortilla, drawing eight lines, crossed in the middle, creating sixteen pieces, labeled '1' – '16'. Stack the tortillas and place them on the tray, in addition to the pizza-cutter and cutting board.

HOW TO DEMONSTRATE:

Place the tray on the work surface. Place the first tortilla, with one line on it and labeled '1' and '2', onto the cutting board. Use the Pizza-cutter to roll along the line, cutting the tortilla in half. Show the child the two pieces saying the numbers '1' and '2'. Now, move your work aside and let the child try with the next tortilla, explain to the child to cut along both lines.

PURPOSE:

This activity helps with motor skills and teaches the child to use a kitchen tool. It also helps the child learn the concept of halves and correlation of numbers.

Wrapping a Gift

SUPPLIES:

- Tray
- Small box
- Pieces of wrapping or newspaper
- Tape

PREPARE:

Prepare the activity by precutting the paper to fit the box. Place all the items on the tray. Set the tray activity in the work area.

HOW TO DEMONSTRATE ACTIVITY:

Lay the paper out flat and place the small box in the center. Raise the side of the paper up so that the edge meets the center of the top of the box. Place a piece of tape there to hold it. Raise up the edge of the paper on the opposite side to meet the center of the top where the previous paper edge is, and tape it there. Now turn the present so that an unfolded end is facing you. Fold down the top edge of paper until it meets the box and tape. Fold in the 2 side edges of the paper and tape. Next, fold up the bottom edge and tape. Spin the present around so the last unfolded side faces you. Repeat the steps you previously did for the other side. Reset the activity by ripping the paper from the package until the box is bare once again.

PURPOSE:

Wrapping a gift helps the child learn patience and works on fine motor skills while developing a sense of procedural order.

Pin Punching

SUBMITTED BY: Anastasia

www.montessorinature.com

SUPPLIES:

- Paper with printed shape
- Color paper
- Giant push pin for toddler or stylus puncher for preschooler
- Punch pin pad or cork board

HOW TO DEMONSTRATE:

The child uses pushpin to punch holes along a line on a piece of paper. After the whole picture is done, gently punch out shape and glue it on color paper.

PURPOSE:

Direct: punch out shape

Indirect: fine-motor, preparation for pencil grip and writing

Sorting Soft and Hard

SUPPLIES:
- Tray
- (2) Bowls (one labeled 'soft' and one labeled 'hard')
- (4) Soft items
- (4) Hard items

PREPARE:

Prepare activity by placing all of the items on the tray.

HOW TO DEMONSTRATE ACTIVITY:

Take an item from the tray and try to squeeze it. If you can squeeze it and it is soft, say "soft" and put it in the 'soft' bowl. If you cannot and it is hard, say "hard" put it in the 'hard' bowl. Sort the items one by one into their appropriate bowls until all the items are sorted. Reset the activity by taking all the items out of the bowls and jumbling them as you put them back on the tray. Let the child try.

PURPOSE:

This sensorial activity helps the child learn to identify the physical characteristics of objects.

Cutting and Collage

SUPPLIES:

- Tray
- Child scissors
- Large white paper
- Basket with strips of colorful paper
- Glue stick

PREPARE:

Present the activity with all items on the tray.

HOW TO DEMONSTRATE ACTIVITY:

Demonstrate how to hold scissors with two fingers through one hole and thumb through the other. Show child how to cut paper. Place paper on tray and wipe sparingly with glue stick, hold carefully with two fingers and stick to larger white paper, continue to make patterns. Invite child to try.

PURPOSE:

This activity teaches the child to use scissors and glue safely, develops motor skills, and promotes creativity with color.

Cutting Straw Beads

SUPPLIES:
- Tray
- Scissors
- Colorful plastic straws
- Small basket
- Piece of light weight string

PREPARE:

Present the activity with all of the items on tray.

HOW TO DEMONSTRATE ACTIVITY:

Hold 2-4 straws in non-dominant hand and scissors in the other. Hold straws over basket. Place scissors about ¼ inch from tips of straws and cut. Continue cutting in same pattern until a safe distance from fingers. Collect any beads that didn't make it into the basket. Once the beads are cut, run a lightweight string through them to make a bracelet. Invite the child to try the activity.

PURPOSE:

This activity helps the child learn to use scissors and develops motor skills.

Paperclip Sort

SUPPLIES:
- Tray
- Several small containers
- Multi-colored paperclips
- Basket

PREPARE:

Place paperclips in the basket then everything on the tray.

HOW TO DEMONSTRATE ACTIVITY:

Carry tray to work area. Begin taking one paper clip at a time out of the basket and place in separate container; one per color (i.e. red, blue, green, yellow). Continue until all of the clips are sorted. Invite child to try.

PURPOSE:

This activity helps the child learn color recognition and like objects and develop fine motor skills.

Colourful Water Jars

SUBMITTED BY: Eloise
www.fridabemighty.com

SUPPLIES:
- Small jug filled with water
- Empty jars with lids
- Red food colouring
- Blue food colouring
- Yellow food colouring
- A cloth to mop up any spills

PREPARE:

This activity could be presented on a tray or already set up at a table. Although this activity looks very simple (pour water from the jug into jars, add colour, screw lids back on, shake to mix the colour and the water) there are lots of component elements.

HOW TO DEMONSTRATE:

Explain to the child that these materials are so that you can explore what happens when you mix colour with water, and what happens when those colours are mixed with one another. Explain that first you need to fill the jars with water, one at a time. This may engross your child so much that you move no further! When this task is complete (and any spills are wiped up), show them how to add food colouring to colour the water. They can then experiment with different colour combinations to create orange, green, or purple.

Older children will be able to screw the jars shut, but very young children will need assistance before shaking the bottles to mix them.

As a secondary activity, once the jars are filled with coloured water, these can be used for:

- "sun play", looking at what colours they project onto paper when held up to sunshine
- transferring coloured water from the jars into bowls using a pipette
- paint pots to dip brushes into
- the basis for sensory jars to which can be added glitter, coloured beads, sequins, small objects, and thicker paint

PURPOSE:

This activity is fantastic for Practical Life preparation. It encompasses pouring, cleaning up spills, mixing, and unscrewing and screwing jar lids.

Mirror and Shapes

SUPPLIES:
- Mirror
- Basket
- Colorful shapes and figures

PREPARE:

Present with colorful shapes in a basket.

HOW TO DEMONSTRATE ACTIVITY:

Lay mirror down on a flat surface. Take shapes out of basket one at a time, and place them on the mirror so the reflection can be seen. Repeat until all shapes are used. Invite the child to try.

PURPOSE:

Familiarizes the child with shapes and colors while helping them learn about reflections.

Cards and Marbles

SUPPLIES:

- Tray
- Basket full of marbles
- A deck of playing cards.
- (2) Bowls

PREPARE:

From the deck of cards, remove all the jacks, kings, queens, aces, and jokers so that only the numbered cards remain. Place the numbered cards on the tray, along with the basket of marbles and the two bowls.

HOW TO DEMONSTRATE ACTIVITY:

Place the tray on the work surface. Take turns drawing a playing card from a centrally located stack. Collect the number of marbles from the basket the represents the number on the card drawn and place the marbles in your bowl. When all the marbles have been taken, each player counts their marbles and the one with the most wins.

PURPOSE:

This fun little game practices counting and number association.

Sweeping

SUPPLIES:
- Broom
- Dustpan
- A bowl of dry rice

PREPARE:
This activity can be presented on a tray or possibly in a basket.

HOW TO DEMONSTRATE THIS ACTIVITY:
With a pincer grip, take some rice out of the bowl and scatter it in a small area on the floor. Now, with the dustpan place on the floor near the rice, use the broom to sweep the rice into the dustpan. Pick up the dustpan and carefully pour the rice back into the bowl. Now, let the child try.

PURPOSE:
This activity helps the child develop dexterity and learn to keep their environment clean.

Domino Addition

SUBMITTED BY: Mars

www.montessorionmars.com

SUPPLIES:

- A few sheets of light black construction paper
- A dark black pen or pencil that will show when writing on the light black paper
- A white pencil that will show when writing on the light black paper
- Tray

PREPARE:

On the paper, with the dark black pen or pencil, draw 2 large rectangles; one horizontal and one vertical. These rectangles will represent addition problems. Within each rectangle, draw 2 squares with the dark black pen or pencil; each square consumes almost half of the rectangle. Now, with the white pencil, put dots in each square to exemplify a number in an addition problem. Keep in mind that both the horizontal and vertical rectangles will represent the identical addition problem. For example: in one square put 5 dots and in the other, within the same rectangle, draw 2 dots. Each rectangle problem will look like a domino when complete. The dominos in this example display the numbers 5 and 2 represented by the dots. Below each domino, with the black pen, draw a line for the child to fill out.

Place the premade cards, displaying the dominos on the tray with the white pencil. Set the tray down in the work area, ready to demonstrate to the child.

HOW TO DEMONSTRATE:

Count the number of dots in each square and write the corresponding numbers on the line below, putting a plus sign in between the numbers and an equals sign after. Now count all the numbers in the rectangle and display the sum after the equals. Do this for both the horizontal and vertical dominos, coming out to the same sum. Now let the child do the next set of rectangles.

PURPOSE:

This activity demonstrates that no matter the order or position of added numbers, the sum is always the same.

Mystery Bag

SUPPLIES:
- Small cloth bag
- Items gathered

PREPARE:

In this activity, the preparation is part of the activity itself: Take the child out with the bag in hand. Collect small items you find either outside or inside and place them in the bag.

HOW TO DEMONSTRATE ACTIVITY:

With all the objects in the bag, take turns with the child, putting your hand in the bag, pulling out one object at a time and naming the object.

PURPOSE:

This activity helps the child become more familiar with objects in their environment.

Using a Spatula

SUPPLIES:
- Tray
- Child-sized spatula
- Items to flip such as a hackie-sack, coaster, or a block

PREPARE:
Place all items on the tray and present to child.

HOW TO DEMONSTRATE ACTIVITY:
Lay items on the tray flat in single file. Pick up spatula and hold parallel to tray. Slide underneath each item and lift. Items can be set back down or flipped. Invite child to try.

PURPOSE:
This activity helps develop the child's hand/eye coordination and use of a cooking tool.

Buttons

SUPPLIES:
- Tray
- (3) Rectangular pieces of fabric with buttons sewn on one end and matching button holes on the other end

PREPARE:
Place the fabric pieces on the tray and present to the child.

HOW TO DEMONSTRATE ACTIVITY:
With the tray on the work surface, pick up one piece of fabric. Position the button into the buttonhole with the button in your dominant hand and the hole is guided by your other. Button all three then reset and let the child try.

PURPOSE:
This activity helps the child with a practical life skill; learning to dress. Also, it develops hand/eye coordination and fine motor skills.

Mortar and Pestle

SUPPLIES:

- Tray
- Ceramic mortar and pestle set
- Sea salt
- Small jar or other container
- Funnel

PREPARE:

Place all items on the tray and present to child.

HOW TO DEMONSTRATE ACTIVITY:

Set tray with mortar/pestle set and sea salt on the work surface. Place a few pieces of sea salt in the center of the mortar. Use pestle to crush the seat salt and use funnel to put ground sea salt into the jar. Invite child to try.

PURPOSE:

This activity helps develop hand/eye coordination as well as teaching the child to use a mortar/pestle and use of funnel.

Shapes Board

SUBMITTED BY: Diane
www.whenhippostalk.com

SUPPLIES:

- Tri-fold display board
- Felt cut-outs (in a variety of shapes and colors) (2 sets)
- Shape patterns (Metal Inset shapes)
- Sharpie
- Velcro squares
- Ziplock quart bag
- Tape

PREPARE:

Choose the desired shapes of the metal insets. Outline two of each inset randomly on the board. Trace and cut two of each shape on various colored felt sheets. Attach a piece of velcro to each outline on the board and another onto the felt shapes. On the two flaps of the board, create a legend showing the shape and its respective name. For easy clean up, attach a quart size ziplock bag on the bottom corner of the board to store the felt shapes when finished.

DEMONSTRATE:

Select a space to work on. Have the child open the ziplock bag and take out a felt shape one at a time. Find the outline that matches the shape chosen and attach. Continue until all shapes are matched. To clean up, remove each shape carefully from the outline and return to the ziplock bag.

PURPOSE:

This activity is inspired by the geometry cabinet and the metal inset. It allows a child to learn and practice discrimination of form. Younger children will be oriented to the world of shapes and older children will be introduced to various names of shapes — all of which prepare them for the world of math and geometry. Also, attaching and removing the velcro help develop fine motor skills.

Clothesline

SUPPLIES:
- Damp children's clothing
- Bucket of clothespins
- Clothesline hung outside low enough for the child to reach
- Small basket

PREPARE:

On a sunny day, wash the child's clothes, letting them spin but not drying them. Place damp clothes in small basket. Place bucket of pins in the top of the basket and carry it out to the cloth line.

HOW TO DEMONSTRATE ACTIVITY:

Use the pins to secure an article of clothing on the line, making sure to stretch each part of the article out so that nothing is overlapped. Now let the child try.

PURPOSE:

This activity teaches a life skill (hanging laundry), while helping to develop hand/eye coordination, hand muscles, and motor skills.

Polishing Coins

SUPPLIES:

- Tray
- Various coins
- Toothbrush
- Small bowl of baking soda mixed with a little water to make a paste
- Small bowl of water
- Dry cloth
- Child and adult sized safety-glasses

PREPARE:

Prepare the activity by placing all the items on the tray.

HOW TO DEMONSTRATE ACTIVITY:

Place the tray on the work surface, put on the safety glasses, and pick out a coin to polish. With the coin in one hand, pick up the toothbrush and dip the bristled end into the baking soda paste. Now use the toothbrush to scrub the coin. Scrub both sides, and then dip the coin in the bowl of water to rinse. Now, wipe the coin clean with the dry cloth. Now let the child try.

PURPOSE:

This activity is a good hand/wrist muscle exercise, helps develop hand/eye coordination and motor skills, and begins familiarity with money.

Watering Plants

SUPPLIES:
- A small watering can or pitcher
- Plants in need of watering

PREPARE:

Fill the can or pitcher half full of water.

HOW TO DEMONSTRATE ACTIVITY:

Take the watering can to a plant. Hold watering can or pitcher an inch or two above soil. Slowly pour in water until all soil is moist. Now let the child try.

PURPOSE:

This activity helps teach the child care of the environment and can be used to introduce concepts about plant life cycle and function.

To the Point

SUPPLIES:
- Tray
- Basket
- Foam block

PREPARE:

Place basket and foam block on tray and preset on work surface.

HOW TO DEMONSTRATE ACTIVITY:

Pick up basket and go exploring for small pointy objects either outside or inside. You can find sticks, pencils, Q-tips, anything that is small and relatively sharp on the end. Collect the items in the basket, and then go back to the work area. Carefully push the first item into the foam block, and then invite the child to do the rest. After all the items are in the block, display it like your favorite art piece.

PURPOSE:

This activity provides both visual and tactile stimulation and promotes creativity of the child.

Sifting Bees from Bread-crumbs

SUBMITTED BY: Marnie
www.carrotsareorange.com *Carrots are Orange*

SUPPLIES:
- Tray
- Mini honey bees
- Bread crumbs in a plastic bowl
- Small watering can

PREPARE:

Prepare the tray; stir the mini honeybees into the plastic bowl with the breadcrumbs. Place the tray with the bowl of bees and breadcrumbs along with the watering can on the work area.

HOW TO DEMONSTRATE:

Demonstrate how to find the bees, remove them from the bowl, and place them into the watering can until only breadcrumbs remain in the plastic bowl. Point out that there are only bees in the watering can and only breadcrumbs in the bowl. Reset the activity and let the child give it a try.

PURPOSE:

This activity improves the child's object discrimination skills and dexterity.

Body Parts

SUPPLIES:

- Tray
- Print outs of a human body (this can be as detailed or simple as you wish based on the child's level of understanding)
- Construction paper
- Marker
- Scissors
- Glue stick
- Small basket or container

PREPARE:

Prepare the activity by cutting around the outside edge of the human bodies with the scissors. Now lay the bodies down flat on the construction paper and trace the outlines with a contrasting marker. Now use the scissors again to cut out the body into sections (head, arms, feet, legs... again as detailed as you want). Place the sections in the basket along with the glue stick. Place the papers with the outlines and the basket with the parts and glue stick on the tray and present to child.

HOW TO DEMONSTRATE ACTIVITY:

Place the tray on the work surface. Pull out a piece of paper with an outline and lay out the glue stick to the side. Pick a body part out of the basket, introduce the part ("This is a leg"), and glue it to the appropriate spot of the outline. Continue until the outline is filled with body parts creating a complete person. Now let the child try.

PURPOSE:

This activity helps the child gain familiarity with body parts. It is highly adaptable to other things as well, such as 'parts of a fish' or 'parts of a cell'.

Counting with Fingers

SUPPLIES:
- Tray
- Construction paper
- Marker

PREPARE:
Place the construction paper and marker on the tray. Present to the child on the work surface.

HOW TO DEMONSTRATE ACTIVITY:
Lay a piece of paper out and place your hand on top. Trace your hand with the marker. Remove your hand and write the numbers 1, 2, 3, 4, and 5 on the fingers. Now trace your other hand and write the numbers 6, 7, 8, 9, and 10 on them. Now show the child your hands and count your real fingers 1-10. Now let the child try.

PURPOSE:
This activity helps the child with beginner counting skills also to understand how many fingers they have.

Making Lemonade

SUPPLIES:

- Tray
- (4) Cups of cold water in a pitcher
- (4) Lemons
- (2/3) Cup of sugar
- Small depression-style juicer
- Wooden spoon

PREPARE:

Prepare the activity by washing the lemons and cutting each lemon in half. Place all items on tray and present to the child on the work surface.

HOW TO DEMONSTRATE ACTIVITY:

Take one lemon half and place it on top of the juicer with the rind facing up. Using the palm of your dominant hand, press down firmly on the lemon half and twist to extract the juice. Remove the lemon half and discard. Repeat for three more lemon halves. Pour the juice into the pitcher. Add 1/3 cup of sugar to the pitcher and stir with wooden spoon. Now let the child repeat with the remaining ingredients. Pour over ice and enjoy!

PURPOSE:

This activity is a useful wrist/hand exercise, which can lead into a life-skill (cooking).

Window Cleaning

SUPPLIES:
- Child-sized caddy or tray
- Small spray bottle
- (4) Dry cloths
- Small sponge

PREPARE:
Prepare the activity by placing all items in the caddy.

HOW TO DEMONSTRATE ACTIVITY:
Carry caddy full of items to a window or glass door. Spray window with water or windows cleaner in bottle, use sponge to remove liquid from glass, use dry cloth to finish removing liquid and streaks.

PURPOSE:
This activity teaches care of the environment and is a good hand/wrist/eye exercise, helping in the development of gross motor skills.

Washing a Table

SUBMITTED BY: Diane
www.whenhippostalk.com

SUPPLIES:

- Tray
- Mat
- Sponge
- Scrub brush
- Bowl (with a drop of dish soap and some water)
- Water
- Towel
- Apron

PREPARE:

Select a table to clean. Wear an apron. Move the chair to another location. Take the mat and lay it on the floor. Using the tray, show the child the following materials and lay each one out in order of use on the floor: bowl, scrub brush, towel, and sponge.

HOW TO DEMONSTRATE:

Wet the sponge in the sink and wipe the table from left to right. Dip the scrub brush into the bowl with dish soap. Brush the surface of the table from left to right, top to bottom, beginning with small circular movements — like lower case "e" — around the edges. Then, gradually increase the movements around the middle spaces. Rinse the brush in the sink and return it to the tray. Take the sponge and soak it in the water. Squeeze it out and begin wiping the table from top to bottom and left to right (repeat if necessary). Use the towel to dry the surface. Take the sponge and wipe any spills on the floor. Return the tray to the sink and rinse each of the materials. Remove the apron.

PURPOSE:

This activity is a great way to teach the child how to clean a table and wipe up spills. It also teaches them logical sequencing of events and proper control of movements. The circular movements made are also indirect preparations for writing cursive letters.

Sand Garden

SUPPLIES:

- Deep tray
- Wood/bamboo rake
- Sand (fill the tray ½ full)
- Rocks

PREPARE:

Place all items on tray.

HOW TO DEMONSTRATE ACTIVITY:

Use the rake to create different patterns in the sand and place the rocks in different locations to your liking. Let the child try.

PURPOSE:

This is a good calming activity, which can start conversations about different cultures. It sparks creativity and imagination.

Hammering

SUPPLIES:

- Tray
- Thick foam block
- Child-sized hammer
- Gutter nails
- Eye protection

PREPARE:

Place all items on the tray and present to the child on the work surface.

HOW TO DEMONSTRATE ACTIVITY:

Wear eye protection and hold the hammer in the dominant hand. Hold the nail with the sharp side toward the foam. Hammer the nail into the foam. Let the child try.

PURPOSE:

This activity helps the child learn a life-skill (hammering) and helps develop hand/eye coordination.

Mail Cards

SUPPLIES:
- Tray
- Basket of envelopes
- Writing pencil
- Cards or drawing on paper
- Stamps

PREPARE:
Prepare the activity by pre-writing names and addresses of family and/or friends on the envelopes and filling out the 'from' address information. Place all of the items on the tray then carry the tray to the work surface.

HOW TO DEMONSTRATE ACTIVITY:
Identify the friend/family you want to write to ("I want to send a card to Papa"). Pick a card to send, sign the bottom and let the child sign as well, and place it in the appropriate envelope and seal. Have the child follow you to the mailbox where you place the card inside (make sure flag is up). Invite child to try.

PURPOSE:
This activity teaches a life skill (mailing letters and cards). It touches on writing and social skills as well.

Organizing Stamps

SUBMITTED BY: Anastasia
www.montessorinature.com

Montessori Nature

SUPPLIES:

- Tray
- Stamp album
- Tweezers
- Stamps
- Small box for stamps
- Magnifying glass

PREPARE:

Show child every object and introduce him or her to language and purpose of every object. Explain why people use stamps and have a hobby collecting them.

HOW TO DEMONSTRATE:

Place stamps on the left side of the album. Use magnifying glass to look at the stamps first. Slowly demonstrate the process of transferring stamps with tweezers picking one stamp at a time and sliding it into a pocket moving from left to right. Point out that stamps may be organized by color, year or country.

PURPOSE:

Direct: collecting stamps, organizing stamps by certain criteria.

Indirect: Learning about different countries; fine motor development; hand-eye coordination, preparation for writing and reading.

Weaving a Canvas

SUPPLIES:
- Tray
- Small canvas
- Colorful string, yarn, or ribbons
- Small flat screwdriver

PREPARE:
Prepare the activity by poking holes in the canvas with something sharp like an icepick or possibly a small screwdriver. Fill the canvas with holes in a grid pattern spaced roughly ¼ to ½ inches apart. Place canvas, colorful string, and small flat screwdriver on tray and present to the child on the work surface.

HOW TO DEMONSTRATE ACTIVITY:
Pick up the canvas and your string of choice. Weave the string through the holes, using the flat screwdriver, if needed, to poke the string through. Now let the child try.

PURPOSE:
This activity is a good hand/eye exercise and stimulates creativity with colors.

Sewing a Button

SUBMITTED BY: Diane
www.whenhippostalk.com

SUPPLIES:

- Tray
- Shelf liner (cut into square pieces)
- Yarn (cut several 15-inch pieces)
- Yarn needle
- Large buttons
- Scissors
- Tape (optional)

PREPARE:

Select a table to work on. Show the child the needle and the yarn. (Tip: Roll a piece of tape at the edge of the yarn (like the end of a shoelace) to make threading easier.)

HOW TO DEMONSTRATE:

Thread the yarn through the eye of the needle so that both ends meet (creating two equal parts) and tie a knot. Take a piece of shelf liner and a button. Hold both together like a sandwich. Show the child the holes in the button. Then have the child thread the needle through one button hole and the shelf liner. Then, pick another hole (diagonal holes make an X on the button and parallel holes make an = sign on the button) and thread. Flip the liner over to continue on the back side. Thread the needle through the third hole, pull the yarn and continue to the last. Once the button is secure and all the holes have been threaded, show the child how to tie the knot. Cut off any extra yarn.

PURPOSE:
This activity encourages the development of fine motor skills, concentration and logical sequence of action.

Tie-dye

SUPPLIES:

- Tie-dye kit (can be purchased in most arts and crafts stores or on Amazon)
- White shirts, sheets, or other items to tie-dye

PREPARE:

Prepare the activity according to directions on kit.

HOW TO DEMONSTRATE ACTIVITY:

Follow directions on kit to twist and place rubber bands on object to be tie-dyed. Use different colored dyes to stain sections of the object. Wait for it to dry, remove rubber bands and wash. Let the child try.

PURPOSE:

This activity is another good exercise in hand/eye coordination and gross motor skills. It combines object manipulation and creativity with colors.

Cleaning Shoes

SUPPLIES:

- Tray
- Dishwashing soap and water mixture (1 part soap to 10 parts water) in a bowl
- Old toothbrush
- Damp cloth
- Pair of the child's shoes

PREPARE:

Place items on tray and preset to the child on the work surface.

HOW TO DEMONSTRATE:

Pick a shoe, dip the toothbrush in the soapy water, and begin scrubbing the shoe in small circular motions. After scrubbing a section, wipe off the soapy water and loosened dirt with the damp cloth. Continue until the entire shoe is clean. Set the shoe out to dry and let the child try the other shoe. Replace the clean shoes with dirty ones as needed.

PURPOSE:

This activity teaches care of ones shoes and is a good hand/wrist exercise.

Leaf Threading

Montessori Nature

SUPPLIES:
- Thick leaf
- Blunt tipped needle
- Yarn

PREPARE:
Make holes around the edges of the leaf using a hole puncher.

HOW TO DEMONSTRATE:
Place leaf with holes in front of the child. Double thread the needle and tie a knot. Start threading for the child and explain that you make a movement pattern - up and down - up and down. Invite the child to continue.

PURPOSE:
Direct: learning to thread using specific pattern
Indirect: fine-motor, preparation for writing

Teeth Brushing

SUPPLIES:

- Mirror
- Sink
- Stool if needed
- Basket
- Child-sized, soft-bristled toothbrush
- Children's toothpaste
- Cup
- Towel

PREPARE:

Have all items at the ready near the bathroom sink and mirror.

HOW TO DEMONSTRATE:

Turn on water, wet toothbrush and apply small amount of paste. Brush inside surfaces of all teeth first toward gum line, one or two teeth at a time in gentle motions. Brush outside of teeth next with short, gentle circular motions; lastly brush all chewing surfaces and then tongue. Take a sip of water, swish and rinse before spitting in sink. Use towel to dry face. Invite child to try.

PURPOSE:

This activity teaches personal hygiene and how to maintain health and appearance.

Funneling Sand

SUPPLIES:

- Tray
- Container of sand
- Tablespoon
- Funnel
- Jar or old clear jug

PREPARE:

Place items on tray and present to the child.

HOW TO DEMONSTRATE:

Carry tray to work surface. Hold the funnel over the jar. Scoop some sand out of the container with the spoon and carefully pour sand through the funnel. Watch it fall into the jar or jug. Let the child try.

PURPOSE:

This activity teaches patience and hand coordination. It prepares the child to start learning to pour liquids making use of a funnel and using a spoon in a controlled way.

Putting on a Coat

SUPPLIES:

- Coat

PREPARE:

Spread coat onto the floor with the front open to expose the armholes.

HOW TO DEMONSTRATE:

Stand or kneel above the collar or hood, facing coat so that it appears upside down. Put your arms as far into each armhole as you can, and flip the coat up over your head and behind your back. Push hands into the ends of the sleeves and shrug coat on shoulders. Invite the child to try with their own coat.

PURPOSE:

This activity teaches a practical life skill (dressing) and encourages independence.

Squeezing Water from a Baster

SUBMITTED BY: Diane
www.whenhippostalk.com

SUPPLIES:
- Tray
- Baster
- Apron
- Two mason jars
- Towel

PREPARE:
Prepare this activity by placing all items on the tray.

HOW TO DEMONSTRATE:
Show your child how to hold the baster by the bulb. Then show her how to suck the water by squeezing and releasing the pressure on the bulb. Move a fully-filled baster over to the second container and squeeze the water out.

It may take a while for a child to learn how to manipulate the baster. A few rounds of practice and a couple of spills should be expected. Keep a towel close by just in case.

PURPOSE:

This activity involves the use of practical life materials that will develop your child's fine motor skills. Though it is simple, it helps the child's hand-eye coordination, concentration, gracefulness, patience and independence. Repetition is important; encourage her to repeat the exercise a few times. It will help her master the skills involved and allows her to gain more confidence in herself as well. It will also build the strength and dexterity necessary to hold a pencil appropriately in the future. Don't forget to have her clean up!

Hanging Clothes

SUPPLIES:
- Tray
- (2) Child-sized plastic hangers
- (2) Children's shirts or sweaters
- Low cloths hanging rod

PREPARE:

Place items neatly on tray and present near low cloths hanging rod or closet.

HOW TO DEMONSTRATE:

Pick up hanger with dominant hand and clothing item with non-dominant hand. Slip one side of hanger into head opening of shirt or sweater and slide into armhole. Use fingers to bring shoulder of other side up onto hanger. Hang on bar and repeat with other shirt. Invite child to try.

PURPOSE:

The child learns a practical life skill (hanging cloths) and independence is encouraged.

Funneling Liquid

SUPPLIES:
- Tray
- Pitcher of water
- Plastic funnel
- Plastic bottle with thin neck
- Small hand towel

PREPARE:
Place all items on tray and carefully present on waterproof surface.

HOW TO DEMONSTRATE:
Sit bottle on flat surface and put funnel down in the neck. Hold onto bottle with non-dominant hand while lifting the pitcher with the dominant hand. Slowly pour the liquid out of the pitcher and into the bottle. Use towel to wipe up any spillage. Invite child to try.

PURPOSE:
This activity sharpens fine motor control, bilateral coordination, and core strength.

Balancing Weight

SUPPLIES:
- Tray
- Set of balancing scales
- Basket filled with objects that vary in weight

PREPARE:

Place all objects on tray.

HOW TO DEMONSTRATE:

Take something from one basket and sit it on one side of the scale. Take something else from the basket and place it in the other side of the scale. See which one weighs more. Add more things until scale balances. Invite child to try.

PURPOSE:

Learning how to use scale, comparing weights of items, learning balance

Bird Nest Tweezing

SUBMITTED BY: Marnie
www.carrotsareorange.com   *Carrots are Orange*

SUPPLIES:
- Tray
- (4-6) Small replica bird eggs
- A pair of tweezers big enough to grab the eggs
- Small replica bird nest
- Small bowl

PREPARE:
Prepare activity by placing all the eggs in the small bowl, and place the bowl on one side of the tray. On the other side of the tray, place the empty nest and tweezers.

HOW TO DEMONSTRATE:
With the tray activity now placed in the work area, demonstrate for the child, carefully picking up the eggs with the tweezers and placing them in the nest.

PURPOSE:
This activity helps fine-tune the child's dexterity and familiarity with birds and their life cycle.

Playing a C.D.

SUPPLIES:

- Tray
- Compact disc
- Compact disk player
- Headphones

PREPARE:

Place cd and headphones on tray.

HOW TO DEMONSTRATE:

Take tray and place near c.d. player. Turn on power to player. Put headphones on ears. Pick up c.d. and open c.d. tray. Place c.d. inside, snapping the c.d. down onto the spindle. Close c.d. tray and push play button. After playing the c.d. for a few seconds, reset the activity and let the child try.

PURPOSE:

Help to develop motor skills and uses logic to establish an order of operations to achieve a goal.

Texture Board

SUBMITTED BY: Diane
www.whenhippostalk.com

SUPPLIES:

- Fabric (choose a variety of textures and colors)
- Wooden or Plastic embroidery hoops (this is the 4″ hoops)
- Scissors
- Cloth pen
- Wood glue
- Poster Board
- Blindfold (optional for an older child)

PREPARE:

Build the board by selecting various fabrics from your local fabric store. When choosing fabrics, try to find ones that are contrasting in texture. This way you can introduce words such as rough, smooth, bumpy, soft, furry and silky. Find fun colors and designs to make it more exciting. It is a great way to teach or review colors too. Place your poster board flat on the table. Loosen the embroidery hoop. Pop the smaller hoop out and glue one side down on your poster board. Repeat for all the smaller hoops. With the larger hoop as a guide, cut out a circle on the back side of the fabric. Lay your cut fabric over the smaller hoop. Press the larger hoop over the smaller one and tighten the screw. Periodically pull the fabric to make sure it is tight. Repeat with all your fabrics.

HOW TO DEMONSTRATE:

Show your child the board. Have her explore the different textures. TOUCH! TOUCH! TOUCH!

EXTENTIONS:

Present the board as a memory game! Place a small sample of each fabric in an opaque bag. Choose a sample from the bag and try to pick the fabric from the board without peeking! Have fun!!!

Composting

SUPPLIES:
- Composting bin
- Compostable rubbish (food scraps, natural yard debris, etc.)
- A bucket

PREPARE:

Set up composting bin outside.

HOW TO DEMONSTRATE:

Gather compostable rubbish from either outside or inside into the bucket. Take the bucket to composting bin and empty the bucket into it. Now give the bucket to the child and let them try, pointing out things that aren't compostable if needed.

PURPOSE:

The composting activity helps the child learn a life-skill and care for the environment.

Changing a Paper-towel Roll

SUPPLIES:

- Tray
- Paper-towel roll holder
- Used paper-towel roll
- New paper-towel roll

PREPARE:

Place all items on tray.

HOW TO DEMONSTRATE:

Remove old paper-towel roll from holder but do not discard. Place new roll on paper-towel roll holder. Reset the activity by placing old roll back on holder and all items back on the tray.

PURPOSE:

Teaches the child a life skill and supports motor skill growth and logic development.

Smelling Bottles

SUBMITTED BY: Marnie
www.carrotsareorange.com *Carrots are Orange*

SUPPLIES:
- (3 or more) Pairs of small bottles
- (3 or more) Pairs of matching scented objects

PREPARE:
Fill each pair of bottles with a pair of scented objects. These objects can be cotton balls with drops of scented oils or extracts, spices, or anything that has a distinct smell.

HOW TO DEMONSTRATE:
The Smelling Bottles Lesson: Presentation I
"Would you like me to show you how to use the smelling bottles?"
Remove the bottles from the box using the 3-finger grip.
Line bottles horizontally from left to right
Pick up far left bottle; unscrew lid and place lid on the table.
Hold bottle below the nose and smell contents. Place bottle on table and replace lid.
Continue until you've worked through each bottle. Offer the child a turn. As child works through the smelling bottles, ask her what the smell reminds her of.

The Smelling Bottle Lesson: Presentation II-IV

Prepare basket with three pairs. Then, for further presentations, add pairs until all are available to the child.

"Let's do some matching with the smelling bottles today."

Remove bottles from tray and position in an inverted V or rooftop with the bottle colors separated by side (left side is one color, right side is one color)

Isolate lower left below the "V". Smell the bottle with the same procedure as in Presentation I.

Select lower right bottle, open and sniff it. If it is a match, move next to control. Sniff the control. Sniff the mate. "These two smell the same. They are a pair." Re-cap and move the pair to the left. Repeat until you have matched all the pairs.

PURPOSE:

This activity aids with sensory development.

Using a Salt/Pepper Grinder

SUPPLIES:

- Tray
- Salt grinder
- Pepper grinder
- (2) Small bowls
- Small pieces of paper
- Marker
- Clear tape

PREPARE:

Use the marker to mark one small piece of paper with a large 'S' and one with a large 'P'. Tape the 'S' to the inside-bottom of one bowl and the 'P' to the inside bottom of the other bowl. Now place the marked bowls and the salt and pepper grinders on the tray.

HOW TO DEMONSTRATE:

Place the tray on the work surface. Pick up a salt grinder and say "Salt". Now point to the bowl with the letter 'S' in it and say "S. 'S' is for Salt." Hold the salt grinder over the bowl with the 'S' in the bottom and grind a little salt in it. Now do the same thing with the Pepper grinder and the bowl marked 'P'. Place the items back on the tray and let the child try.

PURPOSE:

This activity helps the child gain familiarity with salt and pepper as well as the letters 'S' and 'P'. It takes logic for the child to match the two with the appropriate bowls and the smell of the pepper creates a sensorial element.

Sponging

SUBMITTED BY: Diane

www.whenhippostalk.com

SUPPLIES:

- (2) Bowls (Bowl 'a' and Bowl 'b')
- Sponge
- Apron

PREPARE:

Fill bowl 'a' halfway with water. Take both bowls to the table.

HOW TO DEMONSTRATE:

Take the sponge and dip it in the water. WAIT a few seconds for the sponge to absorb the water. Pick the sponge up and (without squeezing the water out) move it over to bowl 'b'. Squeeze the sponge and watch the water fill bowl 'b'. Repeat until bowl 'a' is empty.

PURPOSE:

This activity involves the use of practical life materials that will develop your child's fine motor skills. Though it is simple, it helps the child's hand-eye coordination, concentration, gracefulness, patience and independence. Repetition is important; encourage her to repeat the exercise a few times. It will help her master the skills involved and allow her to gain more confidence in herself as well. It will also build the strength and dexterity necessary to hold a pencil appropriately in the future. Don't forget to have her clean up!

Rubber Band Stretch

SUPPLIES:
- Tennis ball, glass jar, or other favorite shaped item
- Tray
- (5) Rubber bands

PREPARE:
Prepare the activity by placing the shaped item and the rubber bands on the tray. Place the tray in front of the child, ready for demonstration.

HOW TO DEMONSTRATE:
Pick up a rubber band and depending on your child's abilities use one of these two methods to show the child how to use the rubber band.

1. Pick up the rubber with both hands. Holding the rubber band between thumbs and fingers, flip your hands with palms up, allowing the rubber band to slip down over all 8 fingers. Separate hands to create space between them and place rubber band around object.

2. Pick up the rubber band with a pincer grasp and allow the rubber band to slip down on to the thumb which now creates a hook shape. Tuck index finger into rubber and straighten it to create space between it and thumb. Use this action to stretch the rubber band over the item. Repeat for the other 4 rubber bands.

PURPOSE:

This is an excellent activity to exercise dexterity and demonstrate object manipulation.

Storing Washers

SUPPLIES:

- (8-10) Large washers
- A Carabiner
- Tray

PREPARE:

Place objects on tray and present to the child.

HOW TO DEMONSTRATE:

Pick up the Carabiner and a washer. Use your thumb to push in the clip portion of the Carabiner and thread a washer onto it. Do this for the remaining washers until all washers on the Carabiner.

PURPOSE:

This is another good dexterity exercise, combining object manipulation and organizational skills.

Silence

SUBMITTED BY: Anastasia
www.montessorinature.com

Montessori Nature

SUPPLIES:

- Card with word "Silence" and picture from nature
- Mat
- Kinetic sand clock
- Tray
- Mat
- Soft music

HOW TO DEMONSTRATE:

Turn on soft music for relaxation. The child finds silence tray from the workspace. Places clock and silence card on the mat and sits next to it. The child flips the clock over and watches sand grains stack up on the bottom in silence.

PURPOSE:

Direct: the child learns to be aware of their own body and being sensitive to noise.

Indirect: create balance within and relax.

Hooking Carabiners

SUPPLIES:

- Tray
- (5) Carabiners
- A rope tied into a circle

PREPARE:

Present to the child with objects on the tray.

HOW TO DEMONSTRATE:

With the rope in one hand and a carabiner in the other, clip the carabiner on to the rope. Repeat for the next 4 until all carabiners are clipped on to the rope.

PURPOSE:

This is a good dexterity exercise, helping to improve the child's hand strength as they manipulate objects to achieve the goal.

Clipping Fingernails

SUPPLIES:

- Card stock or construction paper
- Scissors
- Finger-nail clippers
- A pen or pencil
- Tray

PREPARE:

Present the activity to the child with all items on the tray.

HOW TO DEMONSTRATE:

Using a piece of construction paper and the pen, trace your hand. On each fingertip, draw a fingernail. Cut out the traced hand with the scissors. Use fingernail clippers to practice cutting fingernails on the traced hand. Invite the child to try.

PURPOSE:

In this activity the child uses dexterity to manipulate an object relating to self-care.

Chopsticks

SUPPLIES:
- Tray
- (2) Bowls
- Small objects such as erasers or buttons
- One set of chopsticks

PREPARE:

Fill one bowl with the small objects and leave one bowl empty. Place bowls side by side on the tray with chopsticks.

HOW TO DEMONSTRATE:

Using proper chopstick technique, move small objects from one bowl to the other until they are all moved. Now let the child try. Help the child position chopstick properly in their fingers if necessary.

*They also make chopsticks that are joined together and easier for small hands.

PURPOSE:

Helps the child develop their fine motor skills.

Texture Walk

SUBMITTED BY: Eloise
www.fridabemighty.com

SUPPLIES:

* None

PREPARE:

To introduce this activity, explain that you are going to go outside and see what textures you can find. Just walking down the street where you live, you will probably see different types of trees, plants, masonry walls, plaster, lamp posts, concrete, metal railings, and many, many more materials and textures.

HOW TO DEMONSTRATE:

The child should be encouraged to talk about what they can see and feel, and can be asked questions such as "how would you describe that?" introducing concepts such as rough, smooth, smoother.

This activity works very well for younger babies and infants who can be carried in arms or worn in a sling, with the parent or caregiver pausing by each tree trunk, wall or bush and giving the child the opportunity to reach out and touch, whilst voicing what the child can feel ("That brick feels rough, but the concrete post next to it feels smoother").

For older children you could prepare a "bingo" sheet of textures to include words like smooth, rough, shiny, spiky, soft, damp, and hard, which the child can then look out for when outside.

PURPOSE:

This simple activity develops both the visual sense, where the child learns how to visually discriminate differences between objects, and (particularly) the tactile sense, where the child learns through their sense of touch. "Although the sense of touch is spread throughout the surface of the body, the Exercises given to the children are limited to the tips of the fingers, and particularly, to those of the right hand."(Maria Montessori, "The Discovery of the Child").

Also, getting ready to go outside – putting on a coat, selecting appropriate shoes – is a wonderful Practical Life activity in and of itself.

Personally, I have found this activity very helpful at times when my daughter is getting irritable or frustrated at home. Just fifteen minutes spent outside looking at a tree and feeling its bark can be enough to provide a change of scenery, some fresh air, and some mindful contemplation. This can do the world of good for resetting and reconnecting tired and cranky children and parents!

Baking Muffins

SUPPLIES:

- Package of your favorite muffin mix.
- Required extra ingredients (usually just milk)
- Mixing bowl
- Muffin pan
- Muffin pan paper liners
- Tablespoon
- Measuring cup

PREPARE:

Prepare for this activity by setting up all the items on a counter or table that the child can reach. You may need to use a stool or learning tower or you could choose to do this activity on the clean floor.

HOW TO DEMONSTRATE:

Pour muffin mix and extra ingredients into bowl and begin stirring for the child...then let the child stir. After ingredients are mixed thoroughly, show the child how to line the pan with liners...then let the child do it. Next, demonstrate how to use the tablespoon to spoon globs of batter into the muffin pan to fill the liners...then let the child do it. Bake the muffins and enjoy!

PURPOSE:

This activity gives a more thorough introduction to cooking. It introduces measurement and exercises dexterity.

Number Matching

SUPPLIES:

- Piece of paper
- Pencil or pen
- Sticky notes
- Tray

PREPARE:

Prepare the activity by drawing numbers 1-10 on the piece of paper. Draw them big so that a sticky note can neatly fit over each one. Next, on the sticky notes draw dots on 10 different notes to represent the numbers on the paper. Place the piece of numbered paper and the stack of sticky notes with dots on the tray and present to the child.

HOW TO DEMONSTRATE:

Demonstrate by taking a sticky note and sticking it to the appropriate number on the paper. For example: place a sticky note with 5 dots on it, over the number '5'. Do this for all 10 numbers and notes, reset the activity and let the child try.

PURPOSE:

This matching activity helps the child's familiarity with numbers and what they represent.

Linking Numbers

SUPPLIES:

- Sticky notes
- Pen
- Tray

PREPARE:

Write numbers 1-10, 1 number per note, at random on a stack of sticky notes and place on a tray.

HOW TO DEMONSTRATE:

On a bare wall, demonstrate for the child arranging the numbered notes in order vertically, top to bottom. Next, reset the activity and let the child try. Then do it horizontally, left to right.

PURPOSE:

This activity sharpens the child's order of numbers skill.

Laundro-Math

SUBMITTED BY: Diane

www.whenhippostalk.com

SUPPLIES:

- Laundro-Math template
- Velcro:
  - (2) long strips
  - (30) small squares
- Laminating sheet/ laminator (optional)
- Ziplock sandwich bag
- Sharpie
- Ruler
- (10) pieces of clothing/socks cut from card stock (5 each of 2 types)
- Number cards:
  - (2) sets of cards numbered 1-5
  - (1) set of cards numbered 1-10

PREPARE:

Prepare the template by turning the card stock to a landscape position. Draw two horizontal "laundry lines" across the card stock — one a couple of inches above the other (upper laundry line and lower laundry line); at the end of each line, draw a small box. Below the second box, draw a larger box. Add a plus (+) sign in between the two boxes. Attach one strip of velcro on the upper laundry line and another strip (same side) on the second laundry line. Attach the opposite side of the velcro on the back of each of the cards then number each card and clothing piece.

HOW TO DEMONSTRATE:

Show the child the laundry board including the number cards and clothing pieces. Have them place the 2 sets of 1-5 number cards face-down. Draw a card and read it. Attach the drawn card to the first box. Select the number of clothing pieces that correspond to the number drawn. Place the clothing pieces on the upper laundry line. Draw another card. Attach it to the second box; select the number of clothing pieces that correspond to the second number and place it on the second laundry line. Count the total number of clothing pieces from both lines. Find the number that corresponds to the "answer" and place it on the large box below.

PURPOSE:

This activity introduces addition in a fun and engaging manner. It reinforces the child's knowledge of one-to-one correspondence and provides a platform for future mathematical concepts. Attaching and removing the clothing pieces also allows for the child to practice fine motor skills.

Other books in the "Montessori at Home Guide" series include.

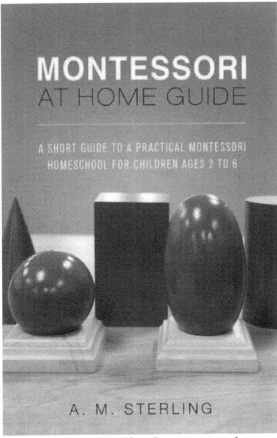

Sign up to receive email updates on new releases at:
http://www.sterlingproduction.com

About the Authors

Ashley and Mitch Sterling are author/indie-publishers and video-bloggers on YouTube known as 'Fly by Family'. When they're not writing or talking to a camera lens, the Sterlings value their time together, in the beautiful bluegrass-laden wilderness of eastern Kentucky, where they live with their two children, Nova and Mars.

Their company, Sterling Production, specializes in producing easy to read guides to help parents get a jump-start on incorporating Montessori inspired learning in their home. These books are created with the busy parent in mind, simplifying their experience with guides that are short and to the point.

Visit our website: www.sterlingproduction.com
Visit our YouTube: www.youtube.com/flybyfamily

About the contributors

Montessori Nature

 Anastasia is from Montessori Nature blog based in Australia. The purpose of Montessori Nature blog is to share ways to incorporate the ideas of Maria Montessori into raising compassionate, independent, happy and successful children. Montessori Nature Blog is dedicated to share fun, nature-centered, meaningful learning experiences, and DIY activities and tips. It offers a wide range of printable educational materials for children, including children with special needs. It also contains online resources which are wonderful time-savers for teachers and parents.

www.montessorinature.com

When Hippos Talk

Hi! I'm Diane, a.k.a. "The Hippo Mum". I'm proud wife to an amazing husband and mom of three wonderful kids- three years old and under! I am also an AMI-trained Montessori teacher with a Masters in Education. I was in the classroom for several years until God blessed us with our first child. Since then, I've embraced my new role as a stay-at-home mom who juggles our daily shenanigans not always with perfection but always with passion. My blog is about discovering joy in marriage, motherhood and Montessori centered on my Master, Jesus Christ.

www.whenhippostalk.com

Ultimate Montessori Parent's Guide

Hello, I'm Chris, founder of Ultimate Montessori Parents Guide, wife of Richard and mum to two Montessori kids – Cooper and Mitchell.

I live and breathe the Montessori philosophy and have spent hundreds of hours in recent years reading all of the fascinating books about Maria Montessori and her successful teaching methods. Those close to me know not to ask any Montessori questions as you can't shut me up once I get started!

www.ultimatemontessoriparentsguide.com

Frida be Mighty

Since having my daughter, Frida, I have become passionate about gentle parenting, and about incorporating a Montessori philosophy into our home. Frida is our first child so we are learning as we go, and I wanted to share our experiences and our parenting journey in the hope that others may find it useful or inspiring.

We live in London, where space is at a premium, and I am particularly interested in how to create an orderly, Montessori environment when space – and money! – are limited. I am a passionate feminist, and believe in raising a daughter who is mighty and can be and do whatever she wants. We work hard to keep our home and her surroundings free from materials which are prescriptive about gender or offensive – another reason I love Montessori – so you may expect the odd blog post on bringing up daughters and feminist mothering.

FRIDA BE MIGHTY

www.fridabemighty.com

Carrots are Orange

This is me, Marnie. I started writing as soon as I could pick up a pencil. Seriously, my mom has stacks of journals from my childhood beginning with one at 4 years old when she had to translate what the heck I was trying to communicate. Thankfully, I have come a long way since 1981. Fast forward to 2016 and I am a family lifestyle blogger from Seattle.

Carrots Are Orange offers you Montessori activities, outdoor learning, parenting, and simple living. This blog is full to the brim with loads of simple living, outdoor learning, & parenting ideas for teachers and parents. Whether you're looking to freshen up your classroom shelves, parenting ideas, or for ideas to bring Montessori into your home, you will find a lot of resources and information at www.carrotsareorange.com.

Carrots are Orange

Montessori on Mars

Sometimes it's "Pitcher Mars", quite recently it's something that sounds like "Teacher Mouse". But mostly I've been called Teacher Mars for some years now. I teach pre-school Montessori, handling children from 2.5 to 6 years old. These days, I'm a new wife and soon-to-be mom. That's basically the short. I didn't digress too much and I didn't use pictures for a show-and-tell version of it. But for all its worth, you can read more about me at www.montessorionmars.com.

Hello,

Thank you for reading our book! We hope you enjoyed it and would love to hear your honest opinion in the form of a review. Reviews help us to improve our craft and to understand if there is interest in future books like this one. You can leave your review at Amazon.com, on the "Montessori at Home Guide: 101 Montessori-Inspired Activities for Children Ages 2-6" product page, in the 'Customer Reviews' section.

Thanks in advance,
A. M. Sterling

Made in the USA
Columbia, SC
09 March 2018